# Heart Medicine

Write your story; heal your heart.

## Kate Bartolotta

For information address Be You Media Group at
**BeYouMediaGroup@gmail.com** or
**www.beyoumediagroup.com**

For information on the workshops and retreats
associated with this book, contact Kate Bartolotta at
**KateBartolotta@gmail.com**

First Be You Media trade paperback edition May 2014

10 9 8 7 6 5 4 3 2 1

ISBN-13: 978-1499384734

To you, the reader.

May you become the hero of your own story.

# Table of Contents

# Foreword

Every drama contains within it a dramatic question. It's often asked by one character to another, and upon its answering, the drama concludes.

The dramatic question is usually, interestingly enough, different from what we first assume it is. Take Hamlet, for instance. Most people would assume that the dramatic question is in Hamlet's goal: will he not simply avenge his father, but do so in a way that assures the damnation of the usurper's mortal soul (which is why the murder doesn't take place when Claudius is praying in the church)? This is Hamlet's motivation, after all.

However, script analysis would suggest that the question is when Claudius simply turns to Hamlet and asks, "How is it that the clouds still hang on you?"

Translating this into a bigger discussion about life questions requires this sort of disclaimer, because sometimes we *think* dramatic questions are simple. Take every horror movie, ever, and most war dramas for that matter. "Will so-and-so survive?" we ask. But we have to think of it like the chakra structure. Survival is a root question. With the next chakra comes the questions related to fulfillment of desire ("Will *a* get with *b*?"). Then, the quest for power ("Who will claim the throne?").

Once we elevate past the third chakra, everything changes. Heart questions are an entirely different level of complicated, because simple answers are no longer in the equation. Everything up until this point has been yes or no, with or without and the identity of the victor—cut, dry, no further questions.

Heart questions, however, beg exploration. They invite deviation and diversion. Can we make stories out of the lower three realms? Surely. However, those often simply form the foundation for the higher ideas. If it was a question of revenge, *Hamlet* would be a two, maybe three act play (if one factors in the political drama going on in the background) at best. Instead, we are drawn through musings on the nature of man and

8

revenge with a few smatterings and dalliances in the columns of lust as political machinations occasionally drift across the stage. Built on a foundation of the lower three spheres, we can finally reach the dramatic question.

This is why we write: once elevated to the heart question, the answers are no longer simple. If they were, we would have answered them and moved on long ago. Even if we were to answer them and end our drama, chances are we'd either started another three along the way or soon will find ourselves spinning into another adventure. When spinning, or in any other state of dis-ease, it's good to have a compass. Certainly, a compass serves better than a map when the landscape is forever changing. A direction is, at such times, better than a destination. Superior to that, however, is giving one the ability to set a destination of their own. That would, however, require that aforementioned compass.

That's what Kate does. She makes compasses. It's not the GPS, because heart questions can't be solved with "Left turn in 500 feet." They require much more care than that. The directions aren't simple, and many times they don't look like directions at all. Sometimes they take the form of musings or revelations. Other times, they're anecdotes. But whatever form Kate's compasses take, of stillness or spinning, they are calibrated such that they point in the direction allowing one to get their bearings.

That is heart medicine, and when it comes to the subsequent writings, I can find no title more apt than that.

— **Kevin Macku**, author and editor

# Prologue

"There is no greater agony than bearing an untold story inside you." — Maya Angelou

From the time we are children, we use stories to make sense of the world around us. Or think further back, and on a larger scale: history, religion, myth. All of our constructs for making sense of life are a form of storytelling.

There are stories we carry with us from our families, from our childhood. We have cultural narratives about everything from gender and race to love and death.

When we open up boldly and look at them, we can take them apart, re-write them where they no longer serve us and write stories of our own. When we take ownership of the stories inside us, they become more than just personal myths. They become a tool we can use to grow, heal and transform our lives.

They become our Heart Medicine.

This isn't a book for you to read; this is a book for you to deconstruct, rip up, write on and use as a tool.

Maybe your goal as a writer is simply to write in your journal and process your thoughts.

Maybe your goal as a writer is to have a book on the *New York Times Best Seller* list, or a blog that millions of people read. Maybe you don't know what your goal is as a writer, or it keeps evolving.

Regardless of what you want to do with your writing, the purpose of this book is to take a look at what your writing is going to do with you, and by extension, if you choose to share it, with your audience.

This is a tool for the writing of your story, both on and off the page.

# Chapter One:
# What kind of storyteller are you?

"Don't forget - no one else sees the world the way you do, so no one else can tell the stories that you have to tell." — Charles de.Lint

Before we dive in to telling our stories, it's worth examining how we've told them in the past. Are you quick to spill your guts with a new friend? Do you keep a tight lip with everyone but those closest to you? Does everyone hear a different version?

Most of us have experienced all of these types of storytelling at one point in our lives. Looking at them clearly is a good starting point if we'd like to move beyond them into creating a new story.

**Four types of storytellers you may encounter:**

**The Hoarder:**

Your story is buried deep within. It influences your choices and your beliefs, but you don't actively look at it or share it with others.

You take in the constant bombardment of media messages—both positive and negative—and let them add new layers on top of your story, rather than revealing the diamond inside of you.

We've all met people like The Hoarder, but maybe were too busy to notice. And perhaps, we've all had times in our lives where we were in this role. Deep inside of each of us there is an essential jewel, a heart story that is so powerful that it could transform the lives of those it touches.

For the Hoarder, that idea is too frightening. The Hoarder is so inhibited by his feelings of inadequacy that he doesn't dare share anything intimate, but merely passes along the stories of others, never daring to open up.

### The Spinner:

You are ever conscious of how your story is being perceived by others. You have many drafts going, many versions to fit different people in your life and different situations. You are in a perpetual state of hyper-awareness of other's approval of you, and shift and change your story to keep that approval coming. For many of us, this is the storyteller we are in adolescence. For some of us, there are certain areas where we feel discomfort and the need to spin things comes up.

This is different than taking a new approach or having a different writing voice for certain types of work. This is a change in storytelling that arises from feelings of inadequacy or shame.

## The Spiller:

You are an open book, yet without any internal control of your story. You lay bare the most intimate parts of yourself easily, but fail to recognize the value of your story, or your self. If there is an opportunity to bare all, you take it. You have not yet found the balance between sharing so that it may benefit others, and learning when to hold back to preserve your own wellbeing.

Sometimes this comes out of inexperience. Truly naked sharing is a wonderful thing when the intention is clearly one of connection. When the driving force behind sharing is a need for validation or a continuation of negative stories about oneself, it serves no one.

We all need a few people in our lives who we can spill to completely, but sharing everything publicly on a regular basis is not necessarily of benefit—to our readers or ourselves.

## The Creator:

This is where we are going to focus. It isn't that any of the other ways of storytelling are wrong—most of us have done at one time or for certain areas of life.

If our goals with writing are to actively move forward on our personal and artistic paths, we need to be facing that way. For many of us, writing generates from a place of discontent, at least initially.

Even in fiction writing, there is a problem that must be introduced and then resolved. Imagine reading a novel that was 400 pages of exposition about the problem and then an abrupt end. It's ridiculous, but many people choose to live their lives that way.

There is value in looking honestly at where we've been. It is essential to take time to be present and fully appreciate where we are. The key is then to set our gaze on where we want to go, and to choose to move in that direction.

You have the power to decide at any point that this is not the path you wish to take, turn the page and write a new story. It's never too late to live a life that makes you proud and write or speak the things you've been holding back.

We get one shot at this. There's no age limit on changing your course, and spend any more time on anything less than what we create from the heart is a tragic waste.

F. Scott Fitzgerald said it best:

"For what it's worth: it's never too late or, in my case, too early to be whoever you want to be. There's no time limit, stop whenever you want. You can change or stay the same, there are no rules to this thing. We can make the best or the worst of it. I hope you make the best of it. And I hope you see things that startle you. I hope you feel things you never felt before. I hope you meet people with a different point of view. I hope you live a life you're proud of. If you find that you're not, I hope you have the courage to start all over again."

Tell your story; tell the one you can't keep inside anymore.

# Write:

Which of these types of storyteller are you most often?

Do you find that it varies depending on the topic?

What can you learn from the types that don't fit you?

Are there areas where you would like to pull back?
Share more?

Do you see yourself as a creator, able to direct where your story will go next, on and off the page?

# Chapter Two:
# Re-writing your story

"We must be willing to let go of the life we planned so as to have the life that is waiting for us." — Joseph Campbell

Psychologist Tim Wilson, of the University of Virginia, made news in 2013 discussing the power of "editing your life stories" as a therapeutic practice.

Through his studies, he found that patients could change their views on events or patterns in their lives in as little as a single session, simply by choosing to re-write the ending, or the belief they held about themselves.

While this is only one tool, what a powerful tool to have available!

If you have made it to adulthood, you probably have some stories from your life that you don't like. You may have stories and beliefs about yourself that you aren't even consciously aware of: roles within a family structure, self-limiting beliefs about your abilities, and stories about who you are.

The purpose of examining these is not to pretend that we haven't gone through difficult things, or even to say we haven't believed those things about ourselves.

One self-help writer, Byron Katie, teaches a process called "The Work" that involves looking at the stories we believe about ourselves and others that are limiting us, and how to let them go.

To go a step further, we might consider accepting the fact that we are going to live out our stories. Creating these stories about life is part of being a human being, and as writers, these stories have the power to shape our lives and the lives of others.

We do not merely write for entertainment; we write to connect and communicate about who we are as human beings.

The key is in bringing our awareness to these stories and deciding to actively participate in the creation of them, of being the hero in our own stories instead of a bystander to whom everything just happens.

From a creative writing standpoint, this feels more obvious. As much as we can feel inspired and some of the best writing seems to flow through us from some larger force, we still inherently know that the ebb and flow of our writing is something we can control.

How freeing would it be if we brought that awareness to the stories we write about our lives?

Imagine you are working in a diner. It isn't particularly satisfying. It's good work. You enjoy the people; enjoy the banter and the pace of the day. But you are a writer. The serving job puts money in your pocket and keeps the lights on, but what drives you is writing screenplays.

If your story about yourself is that you are a server who sometimes writes, you are believing a very different story than the one about a writer who works as a server to pay the bills. It's a small but significant shift.

Imagine you have always struggled with your confidence. Or have always been clumsy. Or are the "shy one." Or fill-in-the-blank. More than any character you will ever put on paper, you get to decide whether those stories are true, and whether or not they will continue. This is part of the beauty of becoming a Creator storyteller. There will be things that come up in your writing again and again; we all have them. When you find patterns emerging and recurring in your writing or in your life, it's a good time to take a look at them. You get to decide whether these patterns will continue, or whether it is time to let them go.

Are you writing this same thing over and over in order to make sense of it? Is it time to take one more circle around it and then move forward? We often ask ourselves or ask of life the same questions over and over, and then one day, the answer emerges and we turn the page.

I remember one early spring day, a number of years ago. It had been what felt like an endless winter—physically and metaphorically; I was depressed. It was the first truly warm day, the first day I could be barefoot in the grass.
It was the first day where I could start to feel hopeful that the winter might be over.

As I stood letting the sun warm me, I saw something floating on the breeze: a small feather. It struck me in that moment, that that is our liminal dilemma in life.

We stand at that threshold in our lives and are faced with a choice: will we be the feather, or will we be the breeze?

When you decide to fully inhabit your life and become the creator of your story, things change. Life still has moments that inspire us, hurt us, and break us open.

But when you decide it's time for your story to go from one of the good stories to one of the great stories, you have to do as the epigraph of this chapter said: let go.

Let go of the safety of repeating old patterns and taking the safe path and instead become—in Joseph Campbell's words—the hero of your own story.

# Write:

What stories do you believe about yourself that you'd like to re-write?

What would be different in your life if you took complete ownership of the fact that you are the one creating it?

Do you feel like the hero or main character in your life, or are there areas where you feel like a bystander?

While there is huge value in looking at the present moment honestly, part of the value is in choosing which direction to go from there. Where are you heading?

# Chapter Three:
# Choose your Tools.

"Being a writer is a very peculiar sort of a job: it's always you versus a blank sheet of paper (or a blank screen) and quite often the blank piece of paper wins." — Neil Gaiman

Personally, most days I write on my Mac Pro and in one of my many journals. I like writing in ink, not pencil, though I have written with a Sharpie when that was all I had handy.

These aren't the tools I'm talking about, per se, but instead the larger tools that make the difference between writing and "thinking about writing."

Most of us have novels, screenplays and award-winning articles written—in our heads. Getting it out of there is an important piece, whether we are talking about creative writing, or even just journaling about what's going on in our lives. Taking the time and making the space to bring our words from inside our heads out into the world are significant steps. Studies have shown that the act of writing a goal down on a piece of paper where one can see it often makes a measurable difference in the likelihood of success. Write it down and put it somewhere you see if often, and you've increased your chance at success exponentially.

A big part of the writing process, as silly as it sounds, is simply doing the writing, one word after another. To accomplish that, we need a few tools.

## Tool 1: Time

There's a funny thing about creative writing; it burst forth effortlessly when you are strapped for time. This is how it works for me anyway— without fail!

There is never the right time to do anything, including writing. There's only now.

Yes, I realize this is Zen and philosophical and there are right times to do many things. It's best to pay the bills before they're past due. It's helpful to put gas in the car before you run out.

But really...there's only now.

Many of us don't have the luxury of stopping everything when inspiration strikes to devote time to writing. And we don't have the ability to bottle up that inspiration for later either. In order to get the words on the page and keep that forward creation momentum, there are a few kinds of time management tools we can use:

## Planned time:

Many writers do this first thing in the morning. I have, at times, but often this is something I do at the end of the day.

If you can set aside even 20 minutes of planned writing time every day, you will get some writing done. The planned time doesn't always yield our favorite work. It's the building the muscle time. It's creating a habit and keeping at it, until it becomes second nature.

There are several books in the suggested resources at the end of this book that have specific guidelines for your planned time if you are looking for more direction as you begin.

**Found time:**

The day didn't go as planned and you have an extra half hour. Write.

It is so easy to use an extra half hour on absolutely nothing, and sometimes that is what we need. But if it's a choice between spending a half hour scrolling through Facebook and a half hour writing, write. Even if it's messy goblidigook.

We don't make progress by only working on something when we feel inspired. Using found time on your writing is like fitting in an extra run or short yoga practice on your lunch hour; it helps build the muscle.

## Stolen time:

Ahhh, this one is the best. You know it.

It's the five minutes stolen time writing in your journal while pulled over on the side of the road because you just had to do it. It's the ten minutes letting dinner burn because inspiration struck. It's the hours up late because you couldn't go to sleep until you had gotten all of it out. And the best way to boost the quality of what comes out during your stolen time? Put the other time in too.

# Tool 2: Space

And then we have the space.

Where should you put your writing? Writing is communication; there are no two ways about it. In *Writing with Power*, Peter Elbow talks a great deal about audience and how perceived audience affects a writer.

If we are talking about writing as processing, however, our audience shifts. Some people feel comfortable processing and being deeply vulnerable with an audience.

There are numerous blogs and bloggers on large sites who have shared tremendously personal things, and there are many fabulous online writing communities.

To me, it comes down to intention. If the intention is to be of benefit to others who have experienced similar challenges, it can be a tremendous thing to share intimately, even with a large audience.

It's also worth considering how it benefits us personally. If we are still in the midst of dealing with an issue, opening it up to the world at large to read might not be helpful.

The dialogue created by the "blogosphere" has the potential to create amazing conversations on important issues. But often, it creates an atmosphere where people, emboldened by the anonymity and distance of the Internet, proceed to vomit out any negative thought conjured by your words (or what's leftover from their therapy session earlier that day).

In your practice of writing, you will begin to find your own comfort level; some things you share with one, some with a small group, and some with the world at large. There is no "right" way, but you'll find your way.

Writers are often given the advice to write every day, but the secondary question hangs in the air unasked and unanswered:

*Then what?*

What do we do with it? Where do we go from there? How do we keep making more every day? What should we be writing every day? What is it all for?

As much as we love to create, if we want to keep that essential spark alive in our work, we need to adopt other practices that help us refuel and restore.

If we consider our creative life to be in equal thirds—create, refuel, restore—about a third of the time we spend on our writing practice should simply be restorative, a practice to process our life events, our relationships, our emotions, and to "clear the dust" when we find we have gotten stuck.

I have a daily Ashtanga yoga practice, which is physical, outward-focused and yang; it could be considered the creative part of my physical practices. Those of us who create, whether it be through writing, artwork, music or any other form, often focus on what we are giving; we focus on output. Without input, eventually the output will cease.

If I didn't eat, or didn't take time to rest and restore, I wouldn't be able to keep up that practice. I would get injured or sick. My practice would suffer. We easily make these connections in the physical realm, but often forget to allow ourselves mental, emotional and creative rest time.

Writing every day is not necessarily writing work that we publish—or even share—every day. I admire the discipline of those who have a shared daily writing practice, in the form of daily blogging or similar; even if you are writing daily in a shared venue, I'd encourage you to consider adopting one or more of these restorative journaling practices as well.

While it certainly is possible to have one journal that encompasses all of these, I like keeping them as separate entities. You might choose a different style journal to fit the different needs—or you might use five identical composition notebooks.

A secondary benefit of keeping them in separate books is that it makes it easier to find what you are looking for should you want to borrow from what you've journaled to add to a larger or new work. Looking back over years of journals can be enlightening as well as fun. It's the writer equivalent of looking back through old photo albums and seeing how you've changed.

Five journals to restore your creative flow:

## 1. Diary/Chronological Journal

If you keep but one journal, it will most likely be this variety, with some of the other elements thrown in from time to time.

A diary is helpful not just to process what is currently going on, but to go back and look at patterns—or see how far we've come.

For many people, a blog or even Facebook has come to serve the purpose of diary-style record keeping. We can scroll back through our "timelines" to see what was going on this time last year, and browse through old moods along with the photos.

While that has the potential to be a great creative endeavor, for the purposes of this journal, we are looking at writing that restores us, rather than writing that creates or connects.

One of the most freeing elements of a diary of this type is the perceived audience (or lack thereof). Even if you ultimately decide to share a portion or the whole of the journal with another person, it begins as a sacred and solitary space.

There is no concern of being misinterpreted or offending anyone. There is no need to be a reliable narrator here. This is your story; you can even re-write your story if you'd like.

## 2. Gratitude Journal

The idea of gratitude journaling has become popular over the past few years, to the point that it's almost a cliché. Call it something else if you need to. Call it the "good book." It can be an ongoing list of things that make you happy or instant mood lifters.

This need not be a journal where you write lengthy entries, but having a separate space to jot down even five things from the day that made you happy is a wonderful thing. For me, I find two aspects of this useful.

First, gratitude always expands our joy. Taking two minutes to put into words things that have blessed our day or that we appreciate is a practice that can impact our entire view of the world.

Sounds too lofty? It's not.

Think again to a yoga practice, or similar physical practice.

The more often you practice a particular posture, the more permanent it becomes in your muscle memory, and the less effort it takes to execute it. Our hearts are muscles too; the more often you take the time to practice gratitude, the more it becomes your instinctive response.

Secondly, having the gratitude journal to look back through can be a wonderful source of inspiration or found poetry. Stuck for an idea? Flipping through lists of moments that made you happy is bound to shake something loose.

## 3. Special Topic/Special Project Journal

This might be one that is used less often, or it might be a good use for a small journal or Moleskine.

It may also be something you want more that one journal for. It also makes it easy when you are taking a break from working on an idea, but aren't ready to part with it.

If you have an area of specific interest or are working on a special project, giving it its own "home," is helpful in terms of both mental and physical organization. This is a more nuts-and-bolts practical journaling suggestion, but one that since I've adopted it, I can't imagine doing without.

Suppose you are considering writing a book on Norse mythology, or epistolary novels, or tea...do you really want to jot down stray thoughts about it in the middle of your diary? How will you find them again?

As projects grow, most people will house notes and writing on the computer, but having a designated space to jot down ideas on the topic as they come up is invaluable. Say you are out at a wine shop and see a vineyard name that would be a perfect town name in your novel—you have a spot for it where you can easily find it later.

This one has some overlap with the miscellany journal, and depending on your current writing needs might easily be absorbed there. If you have several areas of passionate interest or ongoing projects, giving them their own space will be a huge help.

An additional tool for the more visually oriented might be to create a bulletin board or Pinterest board on the topic or project.

## 4. Dream Journal

You know when you wake up at four in the morning from that amazing dream and tell yourself it's okay just to go back to sleep because you'll remember it when you get up?

Yeah, you probably won't. Or if you do—more power to you, it's rare.

In any case, the practice of writing down our dreams or snippets from them when we wake up can be restorative on several levels.

First, you may see patterns in terms of both sleep and dreaming that are affecting your physical and emotional health.

If you are waking up from unpleasant dreams whenever you do _____ before bed, it's worth taking note so you can adjust your habits.

Second, you may find inspiration and insights for both life and writing that your conscious waking mental "editor" would overlook or disallow. Writing down your dreams, even briefly can give you a window to how your subconscious mind is processing your waking life.

It may not always be profound, but over time you will find insights that benefit both your life and your writing. (An additional bonus for those who are interested is that keeping a regular dream journal may increase your ability to attain lucidity within your dreams.)

## 5. Miscellany

This is like the journal version of the junk drawer. You know, that drawer in the kitchen where things that don't quite have a specific home go. This is the Moleskine you keep in your car to jot down a stray thought at the stoplight.

This is the tiny book that fits in your pocket so you can write down the book a friend suggests. The purpose of this journal is largely to keep the other journals true to their own purposes.

This is your "junk drawer," and you may find that some of what starts here may end up moving to one of the other journals or to a larger creative work.

This is the random song lyric that touches you when you are in the bookstore, or a burst of inspiration (as with the dreams, it's best to capture those when they come and not trust to remembering later).

We have seasons where our creative output is on high, and seasons where we shift into nourishing our creative yin and being receptive. Whichever season you are in right now, experiment with this restorative practice of journaling and enjoy its effects on your writing and your life.

## Tool 3: Physical Practice

Even with our writing practices, we are never truly separate from our bodies.

Our posture, our physical energy level, how hungry we are...all of these things will have an impact on our writing.

A seated or walking meditation practice can be a wonderful help to adding clarity to our writing, as well as the rest of life.

For many people, running or cycling is a mentally freeing physical practice.

And yoga, which has a rich lineage of mythology and storytelling of its own, is my personal favorite when it comes to a physical practice that supports my writing.

If you know anything about the chakras, you may think of the throat chakra as a communication center. While it is, the chakras do build on each other as well. If we are having communication issues, it's worth starting with an energy center that's a bit lower: the solar plexus chakra. Our solar plexus chakras are our source of personal power.

If they are overactive, we can be overbearing and aggressive; if they are closed off or underactive, we can be timid or lacking in healthy boundaries.

If we want to be able to speak our minds, we need to start by strengthening this power center near our guts.

There are many different approaches to chakra healing and rebalancing—everything from sound healing, to specific foods to mantra meditation and energy work. One of the things I find most helpful for unsticking these energy centers is to incorporate yoga asanas that activate them into my meditation practice.

A great posture to activate and balance the solar plexus chakra happens to be one of my favorite postures: dhanurasana, or "bow pose." But this is one of many physical activations for our mental processes. Finding a knowledgeable yoga teacher, body worker and/or energy worker will be a great support to your general health as well as your creative process.

*Note:* if you are using your writing to process difficult issues or past traumas, I cannot stress enough how helpful having a guided, complementary physical practice can be for addressing the emotions that arise.

Another consideration is nutrition. While this is a book on writing and creativity and we'll talk about "writing fuel," how we fuel our bodies isn't irrelevant. There is no perfect way of eating that works best for everyone, but replenishing our bodies with nourishing food, rest and exercise has a positive impact on our brains as well.

We don't write in a vacuum where we are able to separate out our thoughts from the physical parts of our life (though most of us have moments where the writing takes over and it seems that way!).

Taking care of our physical health is a key component to being able to create continuously without burnout.

# Write:

What other tools are important to you in your writing practice?

Do your physical practices support your creative ones?

Do you have a space where you feel good about writing? A physical space in your home, office or elsewhere?

Do you have an online space where you feel comfortable writing?

Do you have time set aside for writing, and do you let writing interrupt your day sometimes when necessary?

# Chapter Four:
# Refilling the Well

"Be wild; that is how to clear the river. The river does not flow in polluted, we manage that. The river does not dry up, we block it. If we want to allow it its freedom, we have to allow our ideational lives to be let loose, to stream, letting anything come, initially censoring nothing. That is creative life. It is made up of divine paradox. To create one must be willing to be stone stupid, to sit upon a throne on top of a jackass and spill rubies from one's mouth. Then the river will flow, then we can stand in the stream of it raining down."
— Clarissa Pinkola Estés, *Women Who Run with the Wolves*

What we attribute to "writer's block" in either

creative writing or our journaling practices usually

amounts to one of two things:

1. We have things stuck in the way that we don't want to write.

2. We are running on empty and it's time to refill the well.

Dealing with number one can be simple if we let it out; free writing in a journal can often surprise us in it's content and quality. If you can honestly let go and let yourselves say those things that are in the way (even if the first half is just writing about feeling stuck), you can clear out your mental "junk drawer."

Some of it may even end up yielding useful writing, or lead to new discoveries, but most of it is clutter that we need to clear out.

You know, it's sort of the brain version of that drawer that everyone has that becomes the dumping ground for everything from receipts and clothespins, to pens that don't work anymore and ancient cough drops.

It's stuff like this:

## 1. Shoulds.

I don't mean things we actually want or need to do. Some times we have those little mental pop-up reminders when we've slacked on taking care of ourselves or taking steps towards our goals.

I'm talking about those vague ideas of things we think maybe we should be doing because "everybody else does" or because it fits some ego projection of what life should be like. I should have a bigger house. I should have a newer car. I should have a fancier job title. I should have everything nice and neat all the time. I should be different than who I am right now.

While we strive to let our higher selves emerge and run the show, let's not get caught up in trying to be someone else's higher self...or the sitcom version of what life should be like.

## 2. What ifs.

There is a gap between having reasonable caution and being paralyzed by fear, and if we're honest with ourselves, we know which is which.
Looking before you leap is one thing, but as a friend reminded me once when I was obsessing, it doesn't mean getting out your measuring tape and barometer to make sure you can make the leap.
Worrying about every eventuality for every situation does only one thing: it keeps us from confidently acting and pursuing our dreams. And it doesn't actually make us any more prepared for the outcome.

There are so many millions of possibilities that we cannot even imagine...

We have to decide whether that truth will inspire us or defeat us before we get started. Let go of all of the what ifs, and ask yourself instead, "What's the best that can happen?" and realize that the best might be something you haven't even considered yet.

## 3. Used tos.

Oh, all those old scripts. This is a hard one to let go of; especially with people we've known a long time, or family members.

It's easy to fall into old patterns of what we used to do or how we used to be—especially with people who refuse to acknowledge when we've changed.

If I used to always react a certain way in arguments, the expectation is that I always will. If I used to take on too much even at the risk of my physical and mental health, the perception is that I am someone who will continue to do that.

We cannot change anyone else's mind about these things, but as we change, we can let go of our own ideas about ourselves, and change how we respond.

## 4. If Onlys.

This is the Pinterest of mental junk, and goes hand in hand with the Shoulds.

If only I had X, then I could do it. If only I made more money, then I could find time to do what I love. If only I were braver, I could say what I really feel. If only I lived somewhere different, I could have the life I want.

What a waste.

I call it the Pinterest of mental junk, because I noticed recently how many boards I was seeing with "If Only" type titles.

I saw a fashion board titled, "What I'd wear if I was skinny" and another that seemed to be travel and house images titled, "Maybe in another life." How sad!

Why relegate anything we enjoy to "another life"? It's realistic to make choices, and to say, "Okay, there are many ideas I love, but I am choosing this path for my life," but it's unfortunate that we would eliminate any idea because we think we'd only be able to do it if some external thing changed.

Rumi sums it up well: "Yesterday I was clever, so I wanted to change the world. Today I am wise, so I am changing myself."

## 5. Vague goals and tasks.

You know, ones defined by "more," or "better." I want to write more. I want to eat healthier. I want to be better at communicating my needs. I want to be more organized.

All of these are admirable; none of them are specific. Vague goals and tasks are junk in that they cannot ever really be accomplished.

You can accomplish writing every morning. You can accomplish eating a serving of vegetables at every meal. You can accomplish a practice of cleaning off your desk at the end of the workday.

It's hard to reach a goal that doesn't have a specific destination. It's like the million un-sharpened pencils in my junk drawer when I'm looking for a pen. They have the potential to be useful, but right now, they aren't helping at all.

Taking the time to let go of some of this helps clear the way so that we can delve into the second piece: re-fueling.

If you've been writing for any length of time, regardless of whether or not you publish anything, you may notice that there are times where nothing wants to come out.

It's beyond writer's block; maybe you've even cleared some of the mental junk out of the way and still...nothing.

This happens to writers, as well as other types of artists, when they are not re-fueling. There is something to be said for the writing we do from a place of emptiness, but even that cannot be sustained for long.

Being a writer is not the same being a content-generating robot. While not every piece we write feels full of inspirational fire, when it seems like nothing has felt that way in a while, chances are you are not receiving enough to be able to create anything new.

If we think of the word, inspiration, which implies being full of breath, it becomes simple.

We cannot exhale indefinitely; we need to breathe in or we'd pass out. If we stopped breathing in new air completely, we'd die.

The same is true with our creative breath. We muse be receiving in order to keep giving. We need fresh air to fill us, circulate through us and refresh us before it goes back out on the page. Each of us has our own set of things that best refuel us, but these are a few that seem to be universally restorative. Take time in the writing section at the end of the chapter to add some of your own.

## Nature:

Time spent in nature, whatever the setting, is physically and mentally restorative. In a time when many of us who write are doing it while staring at a computer screen, the combination of fresh air, plant life and natural light will be of huge benefit.

## Reading:

I would hope this goes without saying, but writers need to be readers.

Read books. Read your friends' writing. Read the newspaper if you can still find one. Read poetry. Read plays. Read genres that you don't write. All of it is good fuel.

Play:

I considered including this under the tools section as well; it's just that important.

I love some of Einstein's statements about play, including this gem:

"Play is the highest form of research."

And it is. Research and heart restoration. When I find myself in need of creative refueling, one of my favorite things to do is paint—not fancy canvas "look at me I'm a painter and I know what I'm doing" painting.

Just Tempera paints and maybe some glitter. No agenda. Blowing bubbles is good. Or better yet, watch a small child for a half hour or so.

They just do what they like and approach every moment with curiosity. What will happen if I do this? Maybe I should take off my shoes and splash in that puddle? No specific aim; just play.

## Non-written Media:

For me personally, music and movies have a big impact on my writing and are great writing fuel as well. For others, theatre, dance and artwork may have a similar effect. Seek, find and make a collection of things that fill your heart and make it swell like Thanksgiving afternoon until you are ready to go back to the blank page and spill it all out.

## Write:

Do you notice it when you are running on empty
or almost there?

Are there things you could start planning in terms of refueling to ensure you don't burn out, creatively and otherwise?

What restores you?

Are you actively reading other writers? Looking at artwork? Finding new music?

# Chapter Five:
# Finding a witness

"When someone deeply listens to you
it is like holding out a dented cup
you've had since childhood
and watching it fill up with
cold, fresh water."
— John Fox, "When Someone Deeply Listens to
You."

Having a peer editor or writer friend that you

trust is huge. I have a few friends who I often ask

to go over my work, especially if I feel emotionally

attached to the piece I'm writing.

The key is finding someone you not only trust

with your heart, but someone you trust to be

honest with you.

The friend I ask the most often to look over my work is also the most critical of my work, in a gentle but thorough way.

I had a day where I had something buzzing around in my head, dumped it all into the computer and was riled up thinking it was so amazing and earth shattering.

But...then something made me pause.

I shared it with my friend, and he gently said, "This one is just for you." And that happens. And I needed to hear it. It was something that I was working out internally, and it felt enormous.

I needed his perspective, his honesty tempered with compassion, to protect that vulnerability.

We need to have writer friends who don't just pat us on the back and tell us we're awesome; we need friends who can say, "What if you moved this part up here?" or "What if you tried it this way instead?" or even, "I hear you, and I think this one is just for you."

Writing is a wonderful tool for processing our lives; not all of what comes up is meant to be shared with the world. Some stories are to be kept for ourselves, or merely to serve as a stepping stone to the next chapter; to clear the way for the new story.

Having someone to witness that and help guide you is a tremendous gift. We feel that need for intimacy when we write about deep heart questions; we want to be seen. With those we choose to witness our work intimately, we can be completely vulnerable in a safe space.

The second piece that having a witness brings is validation. While some of us get stuck in chasing validation, to receive it when it's given genuinely is one of the best things a friend can give. Validation from someone we respect says, "I see you. I hear you. I accept you." Even if the response continues on and offers criticism or advice, this initial reception is something we all need, as writers and as human beings.

When we have people in our lives we can share our most intimate, true, and even unpleasant words with, we feel our stories become real to us in a deeper way than we can when we keep them to ourselves.

As John Fox said in the poem from the epigraph, being deeply listened to fills something in us, quenches something in us, and helps us heal.

This is true whether we are tentatively sharing a new piece of fiction, or late night journaling about our innermost thoughts.

Choose at least one person who you trust to share your roughest drafts with completely—both on and off the page.

This is the larger piece of having a witness, especially when we are writing about deep heart centered issues. I have a close friend who talks about how sometimes we share the "rough drafts" with people we love, and sometimes we are too hard on ourselves and feel like we need to have everything figured out before we share the "final copy."

We do this. All of us still have that Spinner storyteller in at least some areas of our lives, and we wait until we've figured things out.

If part of the story we tell ourselves is that it isn't okay to share unless we have everything pulled together, we play hoarder until we feel like everything is nice and neat, and then we share.

The uncomfortable moments of sharing when we are vulnerable and we don't have everything sorted out are important. They are moments of true intimacy that shape our relationships as well as our writing.

Not everyone in our lives is worthy of reading our rough drafts, and not everyone will treat them gently and respectfully.

But when you find someone who does, show them the whole thing, every single time.

One last thought on choosing our witnesses and those we include in the innermost parts of our lives:

"Having a lover/friend who regards you as a living growing criatura, being, just as much as the tree from the ground, or a ficus in the house, or a rose garden out in the side yard... having a lover and friends who look at you as a true living breathing entity, one that is human but made of very fine and moist and magical things as well... a lover and friends who support the ciatura in you... these are the people you are looking for. They will be the friends of your soul for life. Mindful choosing of friends and lovers, not to mention teachers, is critical to remaining conscious, remaining intuitive, remaining in charge of the fiery light that sees and knows."

— Clarissa Pinkola Estés, *Women Who Run with the Wolves*

Sometimes people are in our lives and in our

stories for a chapter, and not the whole thing. It

takes a brave person to know when a chapter has

ended and let go gracefully.

The relationships that last a lifetime and bring out the best in us are the ones with people who want to see us grow. They will be, as Clarissa Pinkola Estés says so beautifully, "the friends of your soul for life."

## Write:

Who is your witness?

Do you have different witnesses that help and listen to different stories or different facets of life?

Do you have different people for your creative work and your personal work?

Do you have a mentor or wish to have one?

# Chapter Six:
# Finding your tribe

"Friendship is born at that moment when one man says to another: 'What! You too? I thought that I was the only one!.'"
— C.S. Lewis

Most people who seek out a book on writing are writers. Obvious, no? But often, we are reluctant to call ourselves writers. That seems to be the realm of someone else. Someone famous. Someone with cool glasses who always has the right comeback. But writers, quite simply, are all of us who write.

As you write more often, and share your work, maybe chose to publish your work, this "imposter syndrome" doesn't necessarily go away on its own.

You have to dig in and ferret it out, over and over, and one way I've found that helps tremendously is finding your tribe. Finding your writer clan— whether it's a local group, other friends that write, a print or online publication…any community of creators, big or small will remind you that you are on the right path, and that **you are a writer.**

Someone recently posted on my Facebook wall that I inspire her. It kind of floored me; it always does.

No matter how much I write, or how many people read my writing and tell me it's affected them, there's still this thing.

This... "What? Me?" and I suddenly feel like a little girl playing dress-up in someone else's clothes, someone else's job. Someone else's life.

Because for me, being a writer isn't about that.

It means that some days I sit here and nothing comes.

It means that sometimes I have to pull over to the side of the road and search for my ragged Moleskine and write and write because I've been mumbling it all out while I'm driving and I just can't wait anymore.

It means that sometimes I do it just to build the muscles because it's what I'm meant to do.

It means that my bedside table is often strewn with waterlogged papers because I got out of the shower and couldn't wait another second to get it down.

It means that when I wake up at 4:30 in the morning, breathless and teary from a dream I roll over and get my journal instead of going back to sleep.

It means that sometimes I lose myself in what I'm writing and don't think I'll ever be untangled. (It means that sometimes I find pieces of myself while I'm writing that I never knew I had.)

What it means to be a writer isn't that we have all the answers or know the right words. We don't have inspiration bottled up to drink whenever we need it. We can't harness or schedule creativity. What it means is more than just that we scribble things down and sit and poke away at the keyboard day after day.

It means that I'm going to get done with this, and more will come. And more. And more. And even when I finish something that wrings me out and I worry that I'll never have anything more to say there will always be more.

All of us who write have this fear that we're imposters or we're amateurs or we'll use it all up.

And the truth is that we are imposters. We are making it up as we go. And it means I will steal from conversations I've had, street signs and graffiti, the person I overheard in line and the dream I had last night. We take all of it, and it takes all of us and we mix it up and pour it out on the page.

And the truth is that we are amateurs. This is no profession. This is love. This is that fire inside that we can't keep in because it burns and burns as Kerouac said, like "fabulous yellow Roman candles exploding like spiders across the stars."

We will see new things and have conversations and dream new dreams, and there will always be more.

Because being a writer isn't just what we do.

It's who we are.

Once you have asserted this for yourself, accepted the challenge and called yourself a writer, what then? How do you write in a way that connects you with your tribe, instead of feeling like you are sending a million paper boats out on an endless sea?

If you want to write in a way that will actually touch other humans, you must open a vein.

There's that thing, that person, that idea that you just can't stop thinking about—that's what you need to write.

When it takes hold and won't let go—that's what you need to write.

When you don't know if you can write about it, it feels like too much, too raw, too honest—that's what you need to write.

When you find yourself mumbling as you drive, in the shower, in your sleep—that's what you need to write.

When you find yourself at your keyboard and it's pouring out of you and you really don't give a fuck how many people read it, because it's true and it's yours and if it touches one other person and is real to them too, it's enough—that's what you need to write.

Write it like a letter that some small part of you needs to remember, the things you have forgotten and need to hear again.

Write it like a love story, to the one who got away, the one you never met, the one sitting on the other side of the room.

Write it like a list, to tattoo on your arm, of all the things you've left behind.

Write it like a poem, to whisper, as you're falling asleep.

Write it as a treatise, a declaration; write it completely—don't leave anything out.

Write it until it's finished, because you must write it, and more will come tomorrow.

Not every day is full of inspiration that rips you up and down or fills you until you burst.

Not everything we write is *that*.

But if we can let go of our audience a bit, and listen to the audience of one, on the inside, we will write what's true. When we make a practice of writing what's true—whether it's about sex or kittens or yoga or politics or vegan soup—then it keeps on coming.

If we practice writing what's true, it doesn't matter whether one person reads it or 1000 people read it. It will have a life of its own, this bit of blood we let out into the world through ink or wires and bytes. It will be alive. It will be real.

If you want to write something that will change the world, write the things that won't stay unwritten.

It is only by tapping into those stories that are from in the space between our bones that we can truly find our writer tribe. If you write what you think people might like to read instead of what's actually begging to come out, you are wasting your time. That's for advertising. Or copywriting content for pay. Both are nice work if you can get it. They'll put food on your table. Neither one will do anything to feed your soul.

When you write those things that make you feel equal parts exhilarated and terrified, you're on the right track. When you write the things that make you feel slightly gutted, or on the flip side, the things that make you start to feel pieced back together, and you share that work? That is how you find your tribe. That is when you find the people who read your self spilled out on the page

and respond with a resounding Yes! Me too.

The journey to finding this tribe isn't without difficulty. Along the way and through trial and error, we learn many lessons.

A few I've learned on the journey so far:

**The more grounded you are in your beliefs, the less you need others to agree with you.**

The first time someone disagrees with you—in print, in public—it's like getting slapped in the face. After writing a particularly controversial article and dealing with the ensuing comments and hate mail, I thought I'd never want to write again outside of my journal. But, after some soul-searching, I realized that getting wound up about what some anonymous strangers on the Internet thought about me probably wasn't worth my time.

When you believe in what you are saying, it still hurts if someone trolls your article or misunderstands, but the disagreement is easier to respond to graciously. How much power do we give the opinions of others? The people we love—sure, those opinions are huge. But random acquaintances, strangers, people who we don't even really like? It's okay to let go of trying to get them to understand where you're coming from.

## There's always something to be gained from feedback, even from negative feedback.

There's a principle that relates to bone growth called Wolff's law; the gist of it is that our bones grow stronger and denser in response to the stress placed upon them.

When we get positive feedback, it's like water and sunlight. The tough stuff, well, that's Wolff's law for our writer backbones. When we are criticized, online or off, it's an opportunity to examine what we've said and see if there's somewhere we went wrong.

And if we examine and find no reason for revision, we can still learn from it. We can learn that other people's reactions don't have to dictate our own. This has been a big one for me, online and off. In fact, I think it might be one of the biggest lessons of my adult life. In our lives, we get to choose whether we are going to set the tone, or be tossed here and there by every passing emotion. We can feel it all, and still remember where we go from there is a choice.

There may always be that piece of us that feels justified in verbally ripping up someone's argument when they've been obnoxious to us in comments or in real life. That piece is tameable. We can choose our responses.

**If everyone likes what you are saying all the time, you probably aren't saying anything important.**

There's a Zen saying "It is the nail that sticks up that gets hammered down." Ugh. But being liked feels so much better! That's the key. When we are so wrapped up in the applause, the booing hurts even more. I've seen writers who seem hell bent on stirring the pot, and others who are determined to stay right in the middle and never piss anyone off. If you write from the heart (and live that way offline, too) it has a great way of weeding out your life.

When we hold back or short-change what we really want to say, we do a disservice to ourselves and whoever's listening (or reading) too. I've found that the more I stick with being authentic, the more I enjoy my life and the people in it. It's hard to hang on to phony or unhealthy relationships when you're being genuine, but the good ones, with people who really "get" you only get better that way.

## There are some things to consider before we dish out "the truth."

There's more to being truthful than just "not lying" and this is important on the page and off. The Sufis taught a story about the four gates that our speech should be able to pass through: Is it necessary? Is it kind? Is it true? Is it timely? There are many times where we might have something to say that's true, that doesn't meet those other criteria. And while our writing need not always be "kind," I think we can all agree that seeing writers consider more carefully whether what they are writing is necessary or timely would be a huge step in the right direction.

The best part in all this is as we work toward finding our balance, as we begin to take charge of our stories—on and off the page—we end up with people in our lives who are a magnificent fit. Some of the best friends I've made, I have made through sharing my writing and finding my tribe.

## Write:

What words would describe your ideal tribe of writers?

Would it be an online community? A local meet-up?

Are you ready to share your writing work (or your journaling process) with a group?

Do you know where to look to find other writers?

# Chapter Seven:
# Manifesto

"And, when you want something, all the universe conspires in helping you to achieve it." — Paulo Coelho

This is what it comes down to, isn't it? When we talk about writing, whether it's in our journals or on a blog or we're writing a novel, the underlying goal comes from the same place. As we discussed in the beginning, the impulse to write is to become a creator. We pull that spark from inside our chests and begin to make a fire. This is why when we read "manifestos" they feel so inspiring and exciting. This is what the creative impulse is: we want that fire inside of us to be made real on the outside.

The Oxford English Dictionary definition of the verb "manifest" is as follows:

"To display or show (a quality or feeling) by one's acts or appearance; demonstrate."

There have been many things written over the years in the spirituality community about manifesting what we want. One problem that seems to resurface and recur when people first explore this idea of manifestation is that they divorce the ideas of intention and action. "If I have the right intentions, things will just work out." Or conversely, "If I just keep at it, my 'intentions' don't really matter; eventually I'll succeed."

The reality is that there is a partnership needed between these elements. We need to find a synchronicity between our internal dreams and the external steps we take toward them.

Having a vision board, journaling about one's goals, and using affirmations are all wonderful tools to help keep a positive focus on where we are headed. They are the map. If I have a map of where I want to go, and simply sit and look at it on my bed, I'm not likely to ever arrive there.

What's the difference? How do we go from dreaming to doing?

There is a gap between idea and action that is hard for many of us to bridge. There are those ideas that are just passing blips on our radar and passing daydreams; those are fine to leave undone.

But what about those other dreams? The ones that keep us up at night, the ones that are our north star, the ones that live in our bones and keep coming back until we do something about them. To let those dreams remain undone is a tragedy.

If it matters to you, if it's one of those dreams that keeps you up at night, don't just dream about it. Don't just post it on your bulletin board for "someday." Someday is not a day of the week.

So how do we get there? How do we take these creative strands and weave them into a reality? How we bridge the gap between dreaming and doing:

## 1. Take one step towards your dream every day.

Yes, we've all heard the "do one thing a day that scares you," and that's great. But we also need to do the work. Taking one concrete action towards our goals—no matter how small—is necessary. Thinking about it doesn't count.

In order to truly shift towards a goal, we need a physical action, even the action of writing about it in our journals. When we take physical action towards a goal, we create new connections in the brain in a way that just sitting and thinking about it cannot accomplish. These simple actions are how we change our lives.

## 2. Tell someone your dream.

Commit. This is a tough piece. I know I have had ideas that I tell people about, and then feel silly when I don't follow through or it doesn't work out. It happens. Dreams evolve, and sometimes we find as we grow the dreams we once had aren't a fit anymore. Find at least one person who you trust to both encourage you and keep you accountable. Choose someone who will be compassionately honest with you and who believes in you.

## 3. Make it visible.

Again, if we keep our dreams all in our heads, we take the risk that they will stay there permanently. Write it down and put it where you see it often.

This isn't to say, "make a vision board and it will all work out." Making a physical representation of our dreams that we see often is not the end. It is a tangible reminder of where we are headed. It is a call to action, not the action itself. This helps us have clarity of focus in a way that just thinking about our ideas cannot.

## 4. Use it to measure what you allow into your life.

This is another tough thing for creative people. We see new ideas and new opportunities pop up all the time. Our big dream should be our baseline. Does this new idea help or hinder me from my goals? Is it a match for the message I want to create with my life? Does this new thing resonate with what I am trying to accomplish? If the answer is "no," let the new idea go. If we spend time grasping at every new shiny idea that comes along, we accomplish nothing. If we let it go, and it keeps coming back...then maybe it's time to revisit or adjust our big goals.

## 5. Don't give up.

Easier said than done. There are days, many days, when it seems like even our best idea is a million miles from being attainable. I love reading about Thomas Edison, and his indefatigable drive to invent. We remember his successes and our lives are changed by them; we might forget at times that it took thousands of failed attempts before he got there.

In his own words:

"Many of life's failures are people who did not realize how close they were to success when they gave up."

When you feel like you want to give up, take one more small step. Talk to the person you've chosen to keep you accountable. Take a look at what you've planned so far. See if there is anything in your life that is acting as an obstacle instead of a stepping-stone, and adjust accordingly. Be open to the idea that dreams evolve, and a dream we have one day may be the boat that carries us out onto the ocean of a much bigger journey.

The closing writing assignment is to write your own manifesto, or the first of many. Or a manifesto that only fits for today, to be replaced tomorrow with what tomorrow holds.

Here is one of mine.

## An Alchemist Manifesto

I believe.

That in and of itself is important. There's what we
think. There's what we know. But then, there's
what we believe. Look at science; I love science
and all it represents. And then there's faith—the
things we choose to believe. And in the in
between space, where they overlap, it looks a little
like alchemy.

The best things in life are in this gap, this
alchemical space where we take what we know to
be true and what we hope to be true and we make

our lives. We put it all together and mix it up and the result is what we believe; it's our manifesto.

I believe in this alchemy. I believe that the space between fact and mystery is a beautiful place to play.

I believe that life isn't just what happens to us, it's what we make, it's who we meet. It's the blissful mixture of the cards we draw and the way we lay them.

I believe in the power of words. Words are where this alchemy begins. We take them, shape them, and send them out into the world, like little paper boats on the water. I believe our words have a ripple effect that changes the world, and as such, we should choose them wisely.

I believe in silence. I believe the way we are silent together is a great measure of a friendship.

I believe in celebrating, celebrating everything. Celebrate beginnings, celebrate endings, celebrate because it's Tuesday and why not.

I believe in never ending conversations, where you pick back up where you last left off. I believe that see you later is better than goodbye.

I believe in honesty, tempered with compassion.

I believe that music is better than any drug out there, and a good long laugh can turn your whole day around.

I believe that a long run on a rainy day will remind you that you're alive.

I believe in having adventures, and that some of the best adventures don't require more than a great conversation.

I believe that staring at the sky is highly underrated, and that if people spent a little more time looking at the stars, they'd be a lot nicer to be around.

I believe in holding hands when you're scared, or sad, or for no reason at all.

I believe that forgiveness is the hardest, best thing you can give to someone who hurts you (and as you give it to them, you give it to yourself).

I believe in making wishes on stars, finding lucky feathers and marvelling at little signs and synchronicity. I also believe that luck is something we make and it looks an awful lot like hard work.

I believe that friendship isn't measured in time or distance, but in the degree to which someone gets your weirdness and loves you anyway.

I believe that family isn't determined by blood, but by who stays, who listens, who believes in you, and who's got your back.

I believe in dancing. I believe it like it's an old timey religion that will save our souls.

I believe in the restorative power of a cup of tea.

I believe in long books, long kisses, and long hot baths that include one or both of the former.

I believe in giving to those who can never pay you back, and then shutting the hell up about it.

I believe the best pictures are the ones that are burned in our memory, because we were too engrossed to stop and take them.

I believe the best stories are the shared ones, the ones we write together late at night and are never done revising.

I believe that sacred isn't a place, or a book, or a philosophy. Sacred is what we are. Sacred is that song our blood sings, our bones know and our hearts keep. *There's nothing more sacred than simply being alive.*

I believe in making art, with words, with paint, with music, with our bodies. I believe that making art is the greatest gift we give the world.

I believe that people are more important than stuff, no matter how you slice it.

I believe that as soon as I finish this, I'll know there's something I've forgotten. But there's only now. And now. And now. It's the only thing that's real. And so I write this now, even knowing that tomorrow there will be some new thing to fold up into my heart or unfold onto the page.

But above all of this, I believe in love.

I believe that love isn't something that's out there somewhere and we have to find it. I believe it's that golden spark inside us, and that when religions cry out "God is Love," they aren't describing a deity; they are explaining that the light in us, that sacred piece of us that has no words and needs no translation, is love. And we write about it, sing about it, cry about it and seek it like it's the freaking Holy Grail, but none of that matters.

Because I believe that sometimes, the best times, we open up enough to share it with someone else. It's not about how much you get, it's about how much you give. And it doesn't matter if it's for a second, or a month, or five years, or a lifetime.

It only matters that we do.

It's why we're here.

## Write:

What's your manifesto?

It doesn't matter if your manifesto is one word, or ten words or a thousand.

Where are you right now?

What matters most?

What do you want more of in your life? What needs to go?

It's okay if you feel like it has echoes of other manifestos you've read, because they all do. They all echo that essential piece inside of us that makes us alive.

# Epilogue

"The feeling is less like an ending than just another starting point." — Chuck Palahniuk, *Choke*

In the beginning was the word...

I once took a linguistic philosophy class, which was the source of many amazing conversations, many existential headaches, and many ideas that are still with me today. My professor, Dr. Judith Perkins, would repeat this statement (which at the time I thought was insanity):

"The real is as imaginary as the imagined."

The stories we tell ourselves, the stories we write, have power.

In the face of the real that seems so dire at times, it is our imagination that makes us wake up and come alive and begin this journey into creating our lives, instead of merely allowing life to happen to us. When someone tells you to "be realistic," never forget that his or her picture of what is realistic is no more accurate than something out of Grimm's Fairy Tales.

This is your story. You are the writer—both on and off the page. Parts of it may feel inspired, and fill you with breath as if they swept in from somewhere else with a life of their own. Some parts will feel like work, like putting one foot in front of the other, or one word after the next. All of it is yours.

Despite what we are told, when we are told to leave childhood behind, there are magic words. Think back to *abracadabra*, that magician's stock phrase, which comes from the Aramaic, "I create as I speak."

Our words have power because they are the genesis of our actions and our internal codex for interpreting the world. Choose and use them wisely, that they might not only create healing and be of benefit in your own life, but that they may in turn inspire others to do the same.

Take ownership of this gift you've been given and become the hero of your story.

# Suggested Resources

Writers need to be readers, period. There are so many wonderful books available to help with the creative journey. Some of these are "writing books," but many more are just books that helped me keep that fire lit and my feet on the path. Telling our stories requires not just instruction in being a better writer, but reading stories, immersing ourselves in stories.

Here are a few that I hope will inspire and enchant you as much as they have me:

- *Stardust* - Neil Gaiman

- *The Little Prince* - Antoine de Saint-Exupéry

- *Peter Pan* – J.M. Barrie

- *Women Who Run with the Wolves* – Clarissa Pinkola Estes

- *The Hero with a Thousand Faces* – Joseph Campbell

- *Peace is Every Step* – Thich Nhat Hanh

- *The Artist's Way* – Julia Cameron

- *Writing with Power* – Peter Elbow

- *Writing Down the Bones* - Natalie Goldberg

- *Zen Mind, Beginner's Mind* – Shunryu Suzuki

- *Mythology* – Edith Hamilton

- *Zen and the Art of Archery* – Eugen Herrigel

- *The Art of the Personal Essay* – Phillip Lopate

- *On the Road* – Jack Kerouac

- *Leaves of Grass* – Walt Whitman

- *Walden* – Henry David Thoreau

- *Howl and Other Poems* – Allen Ginsberg

- *Five Decades of Poems* – Pablo Neruda

- *The Chronicles of Narnia* – C.S. Lewis

- *The Ocean at the End of the Lane* – Neil Gaiman

- *Tiny, Beautiful Things* – Cheryl Strayed

- *Cloud Atlas* – David Mitchell

- *The Alchemist* – Paulo Coelho

- *Stand Still like the Hummingbird* – Henry Miller

- *And Then, You Act* – Anne Bogart

# Online Resources:

For those who wish to share their writing with a larger audience, there are many online resources and writing communities. Finding an open blogging community or publication that focuses on topics you are passionate about is a great way to get started.

**A few (in a variety of content areas) that are full of fabulous writers, editors and human beings:**

www.beyoumediagroup.com

www.elephantjournal.com

www.thegoodmenproject.com

www.rebellesociety.com

www.matadornetwork.com

www.thegreendivas.com

www.yoganonymous.com

www.mysticmamma.com

www.bookriot.com

www.brainpickings.com

I highly recommend submitting articles to publications you enjoy reading. As an editor, it's always obvious when a submission has come from someone who has not read much of the publication. If there is a site, magazine or journal you enjoy, search out their submission policies. You never know unless you ask!

Additionally, here are a few resources to help you as an individual writer:

- If you are looking for direction on getting started with this process or starting a writing tribe in your area, contact me for information about classes and retreats and to receive my newsletter: **katebartolotta@gmail.com** / **www.beyoumediagroup.com**

- If you are working on completing a book and need some coaching toward completion, check out Betsy Chasse's program, *Finish That Book* at **http://betsychasse.net/finish-that-book/**

- If you are looking for information on improving your quality as a freelance writer and connecting with your audience in a larger way, visit **www.copyblogger.com.**

# Acknowledgements

I think if I were to show my gratitude to everyone who had helped me on my journey as a writer, it would double the length of this book.

To my tribe of wild women heart rangers, I love you so. Jennifer White, Bryonie Wise, Amy Cushing, and Sara Crolick, thank you for the role you've played in the creation of my story.

To all of my fellow writers and creators who have inspired and encouraged me on this journey: Kevin Macku (for the beautiful foreword and for always listening to my first drafts—on and off the page), Dana Gornall (for being both my cheerleader and wonderful copyeditor), Charles

Fields (for being my brother, co-conspirator and all around best friend a girl could have), Kerri Crowley, Chris and Jenn Grosso, Joe Bock, Sara Smith, Ariel Temianka, Laura Marjorie Miller, Karl Saliter, Bronwyn Petry, Gerry Ellen Avery, Jamie Divin, Brianna Bemel, Nancy Alder, Jessica Kerridge, Jenn Cusano, Susanna Harwood Rubin, Paula Reeves-Carrasquillo, Sarit Rogers, Renee Picard, Shane A., Rebecca Lammersen, Lynn Hasselberger, Lori Lothian, Waylon Lewis and all of the crew at *elephant journal*, Lisa Hickey and the tireless writers and editors at *The Good Men Project*, Dennis Barone, William Stull, and Judith Perkins, thank you all for being a part of my story and sharing yours with me.

To my parents, for supporting me beyond my comprehension, thank you for never telling me to be realistic and stop dreaming. To my children, Caroline and Finnegan, thank you for being one of the best parts of my story.

To everyone who believed in me and encouraged me and cheered me on whom I've forgotten to mention by name, thank you for believing in me. And to you the reader, if you've read through all of my sentimental gratitude, for you: a six-word story in the tradition of Ernest Hemingway:

*May you live happily ever after.*

**Kate Bartolotta** is the strongest girl in the world. She is the love child of a pirate and a roller derby queen. She hails from the second star to the right. Her love of words is boundless, but she knows that many of life's best moments are completely untranslatable. When she is not writing, you may find her practicing yoga, devouring a book, playing with her children, planting dandelions, or dancing barefoot with her heart on her sleeve. She is madly in love with life and does not know how this story ends; she's making it up as she goes.